I See the Moon

written by **Kathi Appelt**

illustrated by **Debra Reid Jenkins**

Eerdmans Books for Young Readers
Grand Rapids, Michigan / Cambridge, U.K.

Published 1997 by
Eerdmans Books for Young Readers
an imprint of
Wm. B. Eerdmans Publishing Co.
255 Jefferson Ave. S.E.,
Grand Rapids, Michigan 49503
P.O. Box 163, Cambridge CB3 9PU U.K.

Printed in Hong Kong

01 00 99 98   7 6 5 4 3 2

Library of Congress Cataloging-in-Publication Data
Appelt, Kathi, 1954–
I see the moon / by Kathi Appelt;
illustrated by Debra Reid Jenkins.
p.   cm.
ISBN 0-8028-5118-5 (cloth: alk. paper)
1. Children's poetry, American. 2. Moon — poetry.
I. Jenkins, Debra Reid. II. Title.
PS3551.P557812 1997
811'.54 — dc20   96-33232
CIP
AC

The illustrations for this book were done in pastel
and gold leaf on Twinrocker handmade paper.

Designed by Joy Chu

To Wilma and Harold,
who are always there.
And to the memory of Emma,
who is always here.

— K.A.

To my parents,
Russ and Peg Reid,
with love.

— D.R.J.

If I take the wings of the
morning and dwell in the
uttermost parts of the sea,
even there shall thy hand
lead me, and thy right hand
shall hold me.

— PSALM 139:9–10

I see the moon, and the moon sees me.

Does anyone know I'm alone here at sea?

My boat is so tiny, and the waves are so tall.

Who could be listening? Who'll hear my call?

I watch the stars from the bow of my craft.

Who sent these stars to show me a path?

I feel the wind with its whispery tail.

Who told the wind to fill up my sail?

I see the dark is rolling away.

Who brought the sun to meet me this way?

I hear the dove with her song on the wind.

Who sent the dove to lead me back in?

I touch the shore as my boat comes to rest.

Who was as close as my very next breath?

When I set sail again, here's what I'll know:

That God will be with me wherever I go.

God brought me back, snug and safe, without harm.

God kept me close with strong sheltering arms.

My heart is as full as the moon and the sea.

God loves them too. God loves me.